# Pennies, Nickels & Dimes

## A HISTORICAL PROSPECTIVE ON THE AFRICAN AMERICAN ENTREPRENEUR AND THE AFRICAN AMERICAN ECONOMY

### KING L. TAYLOR JR

## Dedication

I would like to dedicate this book to the following people: My father, King L. Taylor Sr., my mother, Gloria Taylor, and my uncle, Leonard Fitzgerald Taylor. My parents instilled in me a sense of pride and always encouraged me to push for my goals.

I have fond memories of my Uncle Sonny (Leonard) and my father discussing the relevance of history as it related to our lives and the world. Therefore, this book is dedicated to all three.

## Acknowledgement

I have not attempted to cite in the text all the authorities and sources consulted in the preparation of this manual, to do so would require more space than is available. The list includes departments of various governments, libraries, industrial institutions, periodicals and individuals.

*Dr. Malcolm Beech*:

Originally from North Carolina, Malcolm Beech attended undergraduate school at Morehouse College in Atlanta, GA. Upon graduating, he accepted a marketing management position with Verizon in Washington, DC. While in DC, he received an MBA from Howard University. He completed his doctoral studies with a MBA in Marketing from the University of Phoenix.

A third generation serial entrepreneur, at 28 years of age he founded a multi-million dollar food, beverage and entertainment company with five locations in Washington, DC. Later, he established a regional publishing enterprise that included public affairs television programming, international video documentaries, community newspapers, regional lifestyle magazines, and statewide travel and tourism guides for North Carolina, Maryland and Washington, DC.

As an avid Civil War historian, he is the founding director of the Cultural Heritage Museum in Kinston, NC, which is dedicated to the 200,000 African American soldiers who fought with the Union in the American Civil War. He is the Senior Vice-President of the National Business League, a national business trade association founded by Booker T. Washington in 1900. Also, he is the past Chairman of the District of Columbia Chamber of Commerce, the largest business membership organization in the metropolitan Washington area.

Dr. Beech is the proud father of four grown children and eight grandchildren. He resides in suburban Washington, D.C.


*Roscoe Crenshaw-Editor*

Roscoe Crenshaw has a B.A. in English, Magna Cum Laude, from the University of Missouri at St. Louis. He is a board member of the Eugene B. Redmond Writers Club and assistant editor of the clubs, *"Drumvoices Revue."* He is an emcee, published poet and former radio host. He has worked as a writer, photographer and or editorial cartoonist for several publications.

Information and illustrations have been contributed by:

Mr. Ryan Taylor

Dr. Kelly Moyers

Ms. Cheryl Peters

Ms. Bertha M. Myers

Ms. Darcell Braylock

Dr. Ronald Evans

Dr. Malcolm E. Beech, Sr. DBA

## What others are saying about this book:

*"Pennies, Nickels and Dimes offer a fresh and sometimes provocative perspective about the economic history of African Americans and how they might be able to improve their condition today. It should provide vigorous debate about the relationship of African Americans to the culture of business and how they have operated at a disadvantage in producing entrepreneurs compared to members of other ethnic minorities."* Professor Gerald Early, Washington University in St. Louis MO

*"Pennies, Nickels and Dimes is an excellent survey of the African-American entrepreneur experiences from slavery to today. The reader will find it informative, insightful and thought provoking."* Nickey L. Jefferson, PhD Youth Entrepreneurship Specialist, Tuskegee University Cooperative Extension Program.

*"Congratulations on writing Pennies, Nickels and Dimes. I read the introduction and a quote from Chapter 1. I was stimulated in these few lines. As an African American entrepreneur myself, I think that we should all hunger for more knowledge about the African American as an insatiable consumer and his plight as an entrepreneur. I have put this book on my priority "to do" list. I will share this information."* Frances Wright, President/CEO Black on Black Love

# Foreword

King Taylor creates a significant analysis of the impact of group culture on approaches to entrepreneurship and business formation. Historically, Africans have always been active and innovative in commercial transactions. African American business and commerce is rooted in the traditions of the Ghana (5th Century), Mali and Songhai Empires (13th and 14th centuries) Founded in 1235, Mali was the world's largest producer of gold. These kingdoms understood the importance of possessing capital for growth and defense. The commercial centers of Timbuktu and GAO promoted trade with northern African countries and Europe. Their medium of exchange for trade was the white shells known as *covries*, although the system of barter was also practiced. The best known ruler was Mansa Kankan Musa, from 1312 to 1337, during its golden age. The Sankore Mosque built in Timbuktu became an internationally known center of scholarship, equivalent to the medieval universities of Europe.

The largest impediments to African American business development and progress have been the institutionalization of slavery and generational racism. America's political system has been used to deprive African Americans of the benefits of public resources, innovative ideas, land, capital and labor. Whether you look at employment discrimination, Black farmer lend losses or government contract discrimination, institutional racism still prevails. The psychological destruction of the Black family and the elimination of Black cultural traditions have made Black unity elusive. African Americans have adopted a western civilization set of individualistic values. This celebration of individual achievement is contrary to the adherence to group goals of eastern civilizations. While many African Americans have individually soared to great heights, the general African American community has taken an immense toll on our economic stability and forward progress. The success of other ethnic cultures can be traced to strong family ties and a reverence for the "collective good." Their ability to share and support other community members is apparent in their successful development of related small retail businesses.

As Taylor points out, the solution for the African American community's future economic growth may rest upon the shoulders of future generations of young African American entrepreneurs. Education opens the door, but entrepreneurship builds the community.

*Dr. Malcolm Beech, Vice President of the National Business League*

# Table of Contents

# Pennies, Nickels & Dimes

## A HISTORICAL PROSPECTIVE ON THE AFRICAN AMERICAN ENTREPRENEUR AND THE AFRICAN AMERICAN ECONOMY

*"We realize that our future lies chiefly in our own hands. We know that neither institution nor friends can make a race stand unless it has strength in its own foundation; that race, like individuals, must stand or fall by their own merit; that to fully succeed they must practice the virtues of self-reliance, self-respect, industry, perseverance and economy."*

Paul Robeson

## Introduction

The lack of ownership in business in America by African-Americans is an African-American problem. African-Americans, as an aggregate, would financially be ranked 8$^{th}$ in the world among countries as consumers. However, we represent only 7 % of American business ownership.-*1*

African-Americans are the second largest consumer group in America, with a combined buying power of over $892 billion currently and likely over $1.1 trillion by 2012. In 2002, African-American owned businesses accounted for 1.2 million of the United States' 23 million businesses.

There are many reasons for this problem and the solutions are apparent, however, the ways to resolve this problem are more complex. We will explore the reasons and come up with some solutions to the problem. This book will address the following problems and solutions:

The historical information on the African-American entrepreneur and entrepreneurship during segregated America, other ethnic groups and their progress, reasons for the problems, and finally, solutions

for the problem.

# Chapter One

## The History of the African-American Entrepreneur

"The desire of entrepreneurs to succeed is stronger than the limitations they often encounter. This was the case with the slaves who became business men in spite of slavery."

The history of African-American entrepreneurship started during slavery. From the first years of American slavery, there were numbers of slaves who were set free. Therefore, throughout the slavery period, until the issuance of the Emancipation Proclamation in 1863, a population of free Blacks existed right along with those who were in bondage. -2

These men represent thousands more who made the best of the bad deal of slavery. American Blacks were fired by the spirit of enterprise and invention that seized Americans of all backgrounds. As skilled craftsmen and entrepreneurs, they contributed to the newly developing nation. The absence of political freedom during the slavery period did not stop free Blacks from becoming successful entrepreneurs and landowners. Despite racial bigotry, they proved themselves to be skilled artisans and farmers. This was possible because of the underlying principle that prevailed among Americans, the notion of the sanctity of private property protected the landowner, whether foreigner, citizen or slave. It was this principle that made it possible for a great many Blacks to prosper and thrive, even during the darkest days of slavery.

*Frank McWhorter* was a slave who lived from 1777 to 1854 and was allowed to run his own business, as long as, he gave a certain percentage of his earnings to his owner. He established a plant where he produced saltpeter, a substance used in fertilizer and as a main ingredient of gunpowder. With profits from his business,

McWhorter bought his own freedom and that of sixteen family members. Such a slave was known to "hire his own time." McWhorter went on, in 1836, to found the town of New Philadelphia in Illinois, where he operated businesses.

Another slave, *John Berry Meachum*, in the early 1800's, was allowed to establish a carpentry business. From his earnings he bought his freedom and that of his family and twenty nonrelatives. After moving to St. Louis, Missouri, Meachum established several small businesses and also built two commercial steamboats to cruise the Mississippi.

*Paul Cuffee* was born January 17, 1759 and died September 9, 1817. He was a Quaker, businessman, sea captain, patriot, and Abolitionist of Aquinwah Wampanoag, African Ashanti descent and a colonizer of Sierra Leone. Cuffee built a lucrative shipping empire. He established the first school in Westport, Massachusetts, to be racially integrated.-3

Paul Cuffee was born the seventh of ten children, the youngest son and free, during the French and Indian war, on Cutthunk Island, Massachusetts. His father, Kofi, was a member of the Ashanti Ethnic Group, probably from Ghana, Africa.

Cuffee used his limited free time to learn more about ships and sailing from sailors he encountered. Finally, at age sixteen, Paul Cuffee signed onto a whaling ship and, later on, cargo ships, where he learned navigation. In his journal, he then referred to himself as a mariner. In 1776 during the American Revolution, he was captured and held prisoner by the British for three months in New York.

After his release, Paul farmed, studied and saved money from his produce sales, then living with his siblings in Massachusetts. In

1779, he and his brother David build a small boat to ply the nearby coast and islands. Cuffee went out alone in 1779 to deliver cargo to Nantucket. He was waylaid by pirates on this and several subsequent voyages. Finally, he made yet another trip to Nantucket that turned a profit.

Cuffee finally made enough money to purchase another ship and hired a crew. He gradually built up capital and expanded ownership to a fleet of ships. After using open boats, he commissioned the 14 or 15 ton closed-deck boat box iron, then an 18-20 ton schooner.

By the first years of the nineteenth century, Paul Cuffee was one of the wealthiest—if not the wealthiest African-American in the United States. His largest ship, the 268- ton Alpha, was built in 1806, along with his favorite ship of all, the 109-ton Brig Traveler.

*Madam C.J. Walker* the daughter of slaves, who, in the early 1900's, turned her dream of financial independence into a hair care and cosmetics business that revolutionized the beauty products industry, creating good paying jobs, and made her a wealthy woman and philanthropist.-4

Born Sarah Breedlove, was an African-American businesswoman, hair care entrepreneur and philanthropist. She made her fortune by developing and marketing a hugely successful line of beauty and hair products for black women under the company she founded, Madam C.J. Walker Manufacturing Company.

Like many women of her era, Sarah experienced hair loss. Because most Americans lacked indoor plumbing, central heating and electricity, they bathed and washed their hair infrequently. The result was scalp disease. Sarah experimented with home remedies and products already on the market until she finally developed her own shampoo and an ointment that contained sulfur to make her scalp healthier for hair growth.

Soon Sarah, now known as Madam C. J. Walker, was selling her product throughout the United States. While her daughter, Lelia, ran a mail order business from Denver, Madam Walker and her husband traveled throughout the southern and eastern states. They settled in Pittsburgh in 1908 and opened Lelia College to train "hair culturists." In 1910, Walker moved to Indianapolis, Indiana, where she established her headquarters and built a factory.

She began to teach and train other Black women in order to help them build their own businesses. She also gave other lectures on political, economic and social issues at conventions sponsored by powerful Black institutions. After the East St. Louis Race Riot, she joined leaders of the National Association for the Advancement of Colored People (NAACP) in their efforts to support legislation to make lynching a federal crime. In 1918 at the biennial convention of the National Association of Colored Women (NACW), she was acknowledged for making the largest contribution to save the Anacostia (Washington, D.C.) house of abolitionist Frederick Douglass. She continued to donate money throughout her career to the NAACP, the YMCA, and to black schools, organizations, orphanages, and retirement homes.

*Arthur George Gaston* was an African-American businessman who established a number of businesses in Birmingham, Alabama, and who played a significant role in the struggle to integrate Birmingham in 1963.

Driven out of Fairfield because of his father-in-law's political differences with the mayor, he bought property on the edge of Kelly Ingram Park in downtown Birmingham, where he moved the Smith & Gaston business in 1938. Gaston extended his business holdings throughout the neighborhood and beyond, opening a savings and loan in the early 1950's, the first Black-owned financial institution in Birmingham in more than forty years. Smith & Gaston sponsored gospel music programs on local radio stations and launched a quartet of its own. In 1954, Gaston built the A. G. Gaston motel on the site adjoining Kelly Ingram Park where the mortuary had once stood.

Gaston died at age 103. He left behind an insurance company, the Booker T. Washington Insurance Company, a construction firm, the A. G. Gaston Construction company (hht://www.aggaston.com), and a financial institution, CFS Bancshares. The City of Birmingham owns the hotel, which it plans to make an annex to the Birmingham Civil Rights Institute, built on the former site of the Booker T. Washington Insurance Company. His net worth was estimated to be more than $130,000,000 at the time of his death. -5

## Chapter Two

### Booker T. Washington and W.E.B. Dubois

### How they impacted the African-American Economy

*Booker T.* and his Tuskegee machine was a major force in the early 1900's in America. Before we discuss the Tuskegee Machine we need to look at the man, Booker T. Washington. Booker T. Washington was born in 1856 and died on November 14, 1915. Booker was an educator, author, orator, and political leader. He was the dominant figure in the African-America community in America from 1890 to 1915. Booker T. Washington was the last generation of Black leaders born in slavery. He spoke on behalf of the large majority of Blacks who lived in the south but had lost their right to vote.

Washington's mother was a slave and his father was White. After being made a free man, Washington worked in West Virginia in a variety of manual labor jobs before making his way to Hampton Roads seeking an education. He worked his way through Hampton Normal and Agricultural Institution (now Hampton University) and attended college at Wayland Seminary (now Virginia Union University). He returned to Hampton as a teacher and, in 1886, he was named as the first leader of the New Tuskegee Institute in Alabama.

Washington delivered the 1895 Atlanta Compromise speech which gave him national prominence. Washington began the speech with the following discussion of interest in industrial progress: He states,

"One third of the population of the South is of the Negro race. No enterprise seeking the material, civil, or moral welfare of this section can disregard this element of our population and reach the highest success. I but convey to you, Mr. President and Directors, the sentiment of this masses of my Race when I say that in no way have the value and manhood of the American Negro been more fittingly and generously recognized than by the manager of this magnificent exposition at every stage of its progress. It is a recognition that will do more to cement this friendship of the two Races than any occurrence since the dawn of our freedom.

"Not only this, but the opportunity here afforded will awaken among us a new era of industrial progress. Ignorant and in experienced, it is not strange that in the first years of our new life we began at the top instead of at the bottom; that a seat in Congress or the State Legislature was more sought after than real estate or industrial skill; that the political convention or stump spearing had more attractions than starting a dairy farm or truck garden". -6

My thought on this is that he believed we should seek economic power before political power. One century and for years later, I would say that his concept of economic power for African-Americans has not been achieved; however, it is the path to true power in America for African Americans.

Again, I pick up his speech towards the conclusion of it and he states "Gentlemen of the exposition, as we present to you our humble effort at an exhibition of our progress, you must not effect over much starting thirty years ago with ownership here and there in a few quilts and pumpkins and chickens (gathered from miscellaneous sources), remember the path that has lead from these to the invention and production of agricultural implements, buggies, steam engines, newspapers, books, stationary, carving, painting, the management of drug stores and bans, has not been

24

trodden without contact with thorns and thistles. While we take pride in what we exhibit as a result of our independent efforts, we do not for a moment forget that our part in this exhibition would fall far short of your expectations but for the constant help that has come is our educational life, not only from the southern stats, but especially from northern philanthropists, who have made their gifts a constant stream of blessing and encouragement."

My thought on this conclusion of this speech is that he is thanking the philanthropists and southern states for supporting the African-America independence in America.

The Tuskegee Machine was a powerful group of supporters for Booker T. Washington and his influential network. The network included powerful Whites, widespread support within the Black business community, educational and religious communities nationwide.

*W.E.B. DuBois* was born February 23, 1868 and died on August 27, 1963. He was a sociologist, historian, civil rights activist, author, editor, and Pan African-Americanist. Born in Massachusetts, in 1888 DuBois earned a degree from Fisk University, a historically Black college in Nashville, Tennessee. DuBois entered Harvard College in the fall of 1888, having received a $300 scholarship. He earned a Bachelor's degree Cum laude from Harvard in 1890. In 1892, he received a fellowship from the John F. Salter Fund for the education of freedmen to attend the University of Berlin for graduate work. While a student in Berlin, he traveled extensively throughout Europe. He came of age intellectually in the German capital, while studying with some of that nation's most prominent social scientists, including Gustav Von Schmoller, Adolf Wagner and Heinrich Von Treitschke.

In 1895, DuBois became the first African-American to earn a Ph.D. from Harvard University. After teaching at Wilberforce University in Ohio, he worked at the University of Pennsylvania. He taught while undertaking field research for his study; The Philadelphia Negro. Next he moved to Georgia, where he established the department of Social Work at Atlanta University (now Clark Atlanta University Whitney M. Young School of Social Work). He also established *The New School* in Greenwich, New York City.

The two great leaders of the Black community in the late, 9th and 20th century were W.E.B. DuBois and Booker T. Washington. These leaders sharply disagreed on strategies for Black social and economic progress.-7

Their opposing philosophies can be found in much of today's discussions over how to end class and racial injustice, Black leadership continues to work on both philosophies today.

Booker T. Washington urged Blacks to accept discrimination for the time being and concentrate on elevating themselves through hard work and material prosperity. He believed in education in the crafts, industrial and farming skills and the cultivation of the virtues of patience, enterprise and thrift. This, he said, would win the respect of Whites and lead to African-Americans being fully accepted as citizens and integrated into all areas of the society.

DuBois said, "Know that Washington's strategy would serve only to perpetuate White oppression". DuBois advocated political action and a civil rights agenda (he helped found the NAACP). In addition, he argued that social change could be accomplished by developing the small group of college educated Blacks he called "The Talented Tenth."

"The Negro race, like all races, is going to be saved by its exceptional men.  The problem of education then, among Negroes, must first of all deal with the, "Talented Tenth."  It is the problem of developing the best of this race that they may guide the mass away from the contamination and death of the worst."

# Chapter Three

## Organizations That Helped African-American Entrepreneurs

## And the African-American Economy

The organizations that helped with the development of African-American entrepreneurs and African-American economy were the following: NAACP, National Business League, the Urban League, and National Minority Business Council. I will discuss each organization's involvement along with their impact on both entrepreneurs and the African-American economy.

The first group will be the National Business League, created in 1900 by Booker T. Washington. The National Business League was founded in Boston, Massachusetts, with the support of Andrew Carnegie. The mission and main goal of the National Negro Business League was to promote the commercial and financial development of the Negro. The organization was formally incorporated in 1901 in New York, and established 320 Chapters across the United States. Later, in 1966, the National Negro Business League was renamed and reincorporated in Washington, D.C., as the National Business League.-8

The League included small Negro business owners, doctors, farmers, other professionals, craftsmen, etc. Its goal was to allow business to put economic development at the forefront of getting African-American equality in the United States. Booker T. Washington felt that there was a need for African-Americans to build an economic network and allow that to be a catalyst for change and social improvement. Also, the League organized that National Negro Business service to help the Negro businessmen of the country solve their merchandising and advertising problems, promoted advertising in Negro newspapers and magazines, and influenced national advertisers to use Negro publications in reaching this extremely valuable group of people with its tremendous purchasing power." The National Business League, for over 100 years, was one of the most influential groups for progress with African American entrepreneurial efforts. The group, for years, was the major advocacy voice for the African American entrepreneur and the African-American economy. However, the group's potency in recent years has experienced some leadership and managerial problems.

The NAACP is an organization composed mainly of American Blacks, but with many White members, whose goal is the end of racial discrimination and segregation.

The association was formed as the direct result of the lynching (1908) of two Blacks in Springfield, Illinois. The incident produced a wide response by White northerners to a call by Mary Ovington, a White woman, for a conference to discuss ways of achieving political and social equality for Blacks. This convergence lead to the formation of (1910) of the NAACP, headed by eight prominent Americans seven White and one Black, W.E.B. Dubois. At the turn of the 21$^{st}$ century, the NAACP sponsored campaigns against violence, encouraged economic enterprise among African Americans and lead voter drives to increase participation in the political process.

In the 1980 NAACP annual convention, a resolution was established calling for the creation of an economic development program within the association's programmatic structure. This resolution adopts the position that the NAACP serve as an advocate for economic parity for African-Americans through the NAACP network of branches and state conferences. The central focus of this project is to advocate on the national, state and local levels for favorable legislation and corporate policies to increase and enhance employment and business opportunities for Blacks and other minorities.

The means by which the project seeks to accomplish its purposes is by encouraging and assisting NAACP State Conferences and Branches to Economic Development Task Forces and Economic Development Committees, respectively. The committee's activities involve seeking favorable legislation and corporate policies that increase minority employment and expand minority business opportunities, legislation and corporate policies that establish minority procurement set-asides and realistic employment goals that take into account upward mobility. The NAACP has always been aggressive in the areas of civil rights and social justice, from its founding to the present day. However, the organization created an aggressive campaign in 1980 for economic parity and independence in America again, another Black organization that worked on changing integrating the dollar and commerce in America.

The National Urban League, formerly known as the National League on Urban Conditions Among Negroes, is a nonpartisan civil rights organization based in New York City that advocates on behalf of African-Americans and against racial discrimination in the United States. It is the oldest and largest community-based organization of its kind in the Nation.-9

The Committee on Urban Conditions Among Negroes was founded in the New York City on September 29, 1910 by Ruth Standish Baldwin and Dr. George Edmund Haynes, among others. It merged with the Committee for the Improvement of Industrial Conditions Among Negroes in New York (founded in New York in 1906) and the National League for the Protection of colored women (founded in

1905), and was renamed the National League on Urban Conditions among Negroes.

In 1920, the organization took the present name, The National Urban League. The mission of the Urban League movement is "to enable African-Americans to secure economic self-reliance, parity, power, and civil rights." The National Urban League is the nation's oldest and largest community-based movement devoted to empowering African-Americans to enter the economic and social mainstream. The Urban League historically has always been dedicated to economic empowerment of the African-American entrepreneur. However, like all of the organizations mentioned, the reasons for better results are many and will be discussed in future chapters. Therefore, we should congratulate these groups for their pioneering efforts, along with the measurable results. These groups had a profound effect on the increase in African-American business throughout the 1900's and, in particular, the years from the 1940's to 1960's, which showed increases in African-American business ownership growth and development. The next chapter will examine the Negro Baseball League and the impact of segregation on African-American entrepreneurs and business. The reason this is necessary is to examine the strength of the African-American entrepreneur and African American economy during segregation. Segregation in America produced some of America's most innovative and creative African-American entrepreneurs. The neighborhoods had all classes of people living together to create a network of professionals, lay people, blue collar, and white collar African-Americans. However, this created some of the most productive businesses in African-American commerce.

## Chapter Four

## The Negro Leagues and Their Impact on the African-American Economy

According to Audrey Edwards and Craig Polite authors of ***Children of the Dream, The Psychology of Black Success,*** "America's early Black wealthy class were invariably entrepreneurs, and their enterprises were inevitably rooted in the delivery of vital services to the Black community, the kind of services that the White community was either unable or unwilling to deliver to its Black citizens.  Early Black fortunes, then, were built on such industries as insurance, undertaking, banking, media, and health and beauty.  In a segregated society where the majority rule would neither; insure, bury, lend money, portray fairly in the press, nor market health and grooming products to its minority population, these needs were quickly filled by enterprising Black businessmen and women."

The Negro Leagues and the Harlem Renaissance occurred at about the same time period in America.  Both institutions had a large impact on African-Americans and the African-American economy.  We will discuss the impact the Negro Leagues had on the African-American economy and African-American entrepreneur.

Owners of Negro League ball clubs varied a great deal in terms of occupational skills, location, and race.  Information about who they were is an important part of understanding the history of the Negro League. Owners were Whites and African-Americans, coming from all parts of the country and from both rural and urban backgrounds. For some owners, baseball represented their only business interest; others operated outside business enterprises as well.  A few operated legitimate endeavors, while others developed questionable outside interests.  Then there were a few who participated in illegal activities.  Baseball ownership provided a way to cover up illegitimate work and gave owners a higher standing in their communities.  Even though many did not make a great deal of money in baseball, owning a team was a great way to advertise other businesses, too, a way to become known and respected in the community.-10

Not all the owners ran other businesses or worked as public officials.  Bill "Bo Jangles" Robinson and Louis Armstrong, for example, also owned ball clubs as a different form of entertaining.  Robinson owned The Harlem Stars before they became the Black Yankees.  Louis Armstrong owned The New Orleans Nine.  Music and baseball represented two ways African-Americans could feel successful and participate in American Society. Often musicians played before and during games to help attract larger crowds.  In Memphis, the Martin brothers brought in groups like The Silas Green Minstrel Show and Memphis Slim, hoping to entice the blues lovers as well as baseball fans.  More opportunities for advancement existed in these areas than in others, so there appeared to be an affinity between the two vocations.  In Pittsburgh, musicians and ball players spent many evenings together after games at the Crawford Grille.  A similar situation existed in Kansas City when the Monarchs played in town. Musicians and ball players were often found together enjoying their leisure time.  A number of the clubs stayed open late so ball players who rolled into town after hours had a place to relax.  Buck O'Neil stated, "The club owners loved it when the Monarch's patronized their establishment because we attracted huge crowds, so they often gave us free drinks."  The players became good friends with musicians like Lionel Hampton, Count Basie and Bill "Bo Jangles" Robinson.

The Negro Leagues benefited from growing racial solidarity as owners stepped in and created new business ventures within developing African American communities. In 1890, fewer than 20 percent of Blacks lived in Northern cities, but by 1910 the number grew to nearly 28. In the same year, over a dozen cities across the country reported African American populations of over 40,000. Chicago had a 50,000 person increase in their African American population between 1910 and 1920. During the same decade, Philadelphia experienced about a 134,000 increase. Detroit and Cleveland followed closely behind with jumps of 35,000 and 26,000, respectively. Other Negro Leagues cities such as St. Louis, Kansas City, Cincinnati, Washington, D.C., Baltimore, Memphis, Birmingham, Atlanta, and Indianapolis experienced similar population trends.

The cultural separatism of the Harlem Renaissance fit well with the growing sense of self help within the African American community. This philosophy carried over into the founding of the Negro Leagues as a necessary step, until the day arrived when all ball players competed against one another instead of in segregated Leagues. Rube Foster believed the main goal of the Negro Leagues was preparing for integration; when that day arrived he wanted athletes to be ready to step forward. Foster also believed that African American ball players had great skill and deserved the chance to show off that talent to the world. Rube Foster turned this idea into reality with the formation of the Negro National League in 1920. He used his own connections in the baseball world as well as his skills as a former ball player to bring this development about.

The Negro League teams would use the following African American businesses: hotels, restaurants, laundries, shoe shine parlors, jazz clubs, barber shops, movie theaters, and churches during their travels.

Former player George Giles said, "We couldn't stay in White hotels, we couldn't eat in restaurants. In most cities there usually weren't Negro hotels." Former player Sydney Bunch recalled, "Down in Mississippi, we'd go two or three days with no bath. We might go to the Greyhound station and wash up a little, but you'd still be stinking; those were hard times." The Homestead Grays once booked rooms at a White hotel through Seay Posey, who was light skinned. When they arrived, the management told them there had been a mistake and that the rooms were already booked. When black hotels could be found, sometimes there weren't enough rooms for all the players. In Harlem, players could stay at the Theresa and Woodside hotels, in Chicago, accommodations could be arranged at the Vincennes and Grand, in Kansas City, you could sleep at the Street Hotel. In St. Louis, rooms could be secured at the Crystal White Hotel, at the Auburn Hotel in Atlanta, the Grand Hotel in Newark; The York Hotel in Baltimore; and the Rush Hotel in Birmingham. In some communities, visiting ball players would be put up in private homes and rooming houses within the African American communities. This created a greater sense of loyalty between fans and players; connections developed that could not have happened in any other way. Staying with a family beat the other accommodations that usually could be found.

Big cities offered a better opportunity to find African American owned restaurants so that team members could eat in peace and relative comfort. Johnnie Cowan, former Black Baron, remembers playing a game one night in Chicago and trying to find a place to eat. After the contest, they found a White establishment that would not allow them entry. The police came to the scene because the restaurant owners expected there would be trouble, and they agreed with management that the restaurant was closed, even though people sat inside eating. Instead of forcing the issue, Cowan and his teammates went down the street and found a lunch counter that served them sandwiches before they left for another town and their next game.

Pitcher Ralph Mellix remembered receiving an average of $2.00 a day for meal money during his career, but it was enough to get by. "I spent $0.45 cents for pork chops and eggs twice a day and had $1.10 left over. With that extra, he could save it, buy something extra or send it to family, as many players did. Even though ball players did not look like they were making a lot of money, in most cases their salaries were higher than salaries for other types of work.

Buck O'Neil claimed he felt fortunate enough to get paid for doing something he loved. "When I started I was making $100.00 a month, with $1.00 a day for meal money. But in those days, you could get breakfast for .25 cents and dinner for .35 cents. We didn't eat more than two meals a day. Cigarettes cost .15 cents and I could go to a movie for .10 cents. So you could operate out of a dollar."

Within their own communities and neighborhoods, the Negro League teams had strong ties and followings. This was part of the great success of the Negro Leagues. The ball players were a part of their communities because they gave so much both economically and socially. The money spent by teams and individual players helped communities economically but the athletes also represented hopes and dreams; a dream of one day being accepted in America, a dream for their sons to one day play in the majors, a dream that things could change for the better. Hope revolved around the athletes because their success meant opportunities for others in different arenas. If the National pastime ever truly became National, then all would be participating on an even field. Race inequities, at least, would have to disappear.

Ball players earned respect as they travelled because they brought something to the communities they visited. They did not just entertain; they brought hopes and dreams; many became heroes for the boys and girls who saw them play.

Buck O'Neil said, "The Black community supported and loved the Monarchs and the team reciprocated. Kansas City was a good baseball town, when the Monarchs came to town everything happened." Games at Muehlebach Field took place after hours of celebration. O'Neil remembers, "Saturday nights 18th and Vine was like a carnival. Everybody would congregate at the Blue Room of Fox's Tavern or the Subway. At the Subway the guys would hold a jam session; the Monarchs were loved and respected and J.L. Wilkinson worked hard to ensure his players lived up to that respect." Byron Johnson played for Wilkinson and remembers being told, "I want my players to look like gentlemen when they step off that bus. I want them to be dressed nice and act nice. You didn't hear any cussing or see us look raggedy and dirty. We represented the Monarchs."

The Monarchs' situation was not unique. When the Homestead Grays came to town the whole neighborhood got involved. Fans camped out at the stadium with picnic lunches, fried chicken and sometimes illicit bottles of whiskey. The youngsters sneaked into games with neighborhood buddies. When the Grays came to town the whole community would be excited. After the games ended, the players still played an important role; they became *role models* for young people. A lot of kids patterned themselves after the

Homestead Grays.  The games gave the young people some hope and something to look forward to.  As one former fan remembers, "We still don't realize what an important part of the community the Grays were."

 At the start of the 1945 season, three Negro Leagues existed, the Negro Southern League (NAL) the Negro Southern League (NSL) and the second Negro National League (NNL), soon joined by the United States League (USL).  Each passing year saw the decline in teams and leagues until only the NAL remained.

 While most believed that the integration of baseball was a good thing, others were ambivalent, because of the loss to the African American business community.  At one point in the early 1940's, Effa Manley of the Newark Eagles claimed that they operated a two million dollar business that disappeared without being replaced.

For baseball, the growing Black population created a market and an audience.  It also brought together players from many areas of the South.  Black businesses developed out of necessity, to meet the needs of growing communities that were not served by white society.

Providing entertainment and reflecting pride for Black neighborhoods forced many to provide for themselves, and black communities set out to demonstrate that they could do so successfully.

With the onslaught of the depression, teams folded.  Leagues died out and a new breed of owner stepped in to save the games. Owners like Alex Pompez, Abe Manley and Gus Greenlee were *number kings*.

They controlled the illegal numbers racket in their respective cities and gave some of the money they made back to their communities. Through ownership of the Newark Eagles, the New York Cubans and the Pittsburgh Crawford's, owning a baseball club also gave them legitimate businesses to cover their illegal activities. The Depression caused a decline in attendance, travel and salaries, thus bringing an end to the first NNL. As a result, a number of teams added incentives; contest, beauty pageants, parades, booster clubs, ladies days, and other events, in an effort to boost fan appeal. This is when the idea of Negro Leagues as entertainers truly developed. Teams like the Zulu Cannibal Giants became popular, while other clubs hired comedians to travel with their teams to entertain before games and in between innings.

What followed is a history of the final years of the leagues from 1945 through 1960. Teams in the various leagues changed from year to year, as franchises moved when teams folded or were sold. Cities with long-term representation were those with large Black populations, like Chicago, New York, Newark, and Cleveland.

A study conducted by the Senate sub-committee on Labor and Labor Management Relations examined American Society from 1940 to 1950, and determined that conditions for African Americans were improving steadily in terms of employment and housing. As Jim Crow was weakening with those improvements, segregation lessened its hold, and structures like the Negro Leagues were no longer needed. As a result, cities with large Black populations lost part of their community's identity when the Negro League teams ceased to exist.

In 1957, the Sporting News paid attention to the Negro Leagues and their declining fortunes. In an article by Doc Young, the magazine chronicled the difficulties the Negro Leagues were having trying to stay alive.  League President J.B. Martin had stopped taking a salary or charging for office space and staff. For leagues with the best young players heading to the majors, it was getting harder to attract fans to their games.  Young indicated the factors he blamed for the Negro Leagues demise: integration, television, the improvement in economic standings of many Blacks, the appeal of other sports, and the integration of other sports and their facilities.

The end of the color line in baseball did not just mean the National pastime had changed, but that America was slowly changing. Signing Jackie Robinson to a Brooklyn Dodgers contract meant that the face of America was shifting.  The way things had always been was not going to continue.  People stood to lose things they had long taken for granted, while others would gain a great deal.  The end of the Negro Leagues marked the end of a long, sad chapter in America's history, a chapter which had made such separation necessary and acceptable, but it signaled the demise of a great institution in the African American community.

## Chapter Five

## Black Wall Street and Its Impact on the African American Entrepreneur

## And the African American Economy

During the early 1900's in a small northern section of Tulsa, Oklahoma a rare group of Blacks built what came to be known as "Black Wall Street." In a 36 square block section of north Tulsa, over 600 thriving Black businesses prospered beyond the imagination. The small town was originally named Greenwood; however it was soon referred to as "Little Africa" and "Nigger Town" by racist hate groups such as the Knights of Liberty, the Klan, the White Camella and others. After it prospered and flourished, it was then nicknamed America's *Black Wall Street* by members of the New York financial district.-11

Several highly educated Black doctors, lawyers, educators, business owners, oilmen, and entrepreneurs actually controlled their own destinies in a society that prevented them from venturing into parts of the city. Strict *Jim Crow* laws were set up and made it illegal for Blacks to go into other parts of the city, except to work for a White family or business. Curfew laws were set up and strictly enforced. At one point something fascinating began to happen, *the Black dollar began circulating throughout the Black community*.

There were several Black millionaires and dozens of wealthy Black business owners who actually made Black Wall Street tick. They owned private airplanes, bus lines, restaurants, general stores, feed and grain stores, beauty salons, real estate companies, night clubs, hotels, a bank, schools, churches - over 600 booming businesses and two theaters, one that held 700 seats!

During those times, the KKK practically owned and controlled the entire state of Oklahoma - the Bible belt of America - God's country, so they called it. But nothing was further from the truth.

The date was June 1, 1921, when "Black Wall Street," the name fittingly given to one of the most affluent all-Black communities in America, was bombed from the air and burned to the ground by mobs of envious Whites. In a period spanning fewer than 12 hours, a once thriving 36 block business district in northern Tulsa lay smoldering - a model community destroyed, and a major African-American economic movement resoundingly defused. The night's carnage left some 3,000 African-Americans dead, and over 600 successful businesses lost. Among these were 21 churches, 21 restaurants, 30 grocery stores and two movie theatres, plus a hospital, a bank, a post office, libraries, schools, law offices, a half dozen private airplanes, and even a bus system. As expected, the group behind it all was the infamous Ku Klux Klan, working in consort with ranking city officials and many other sympathizers.-12

The best description of Black Wall Street, or Little Africa as it was also known, would be likening it to a mini-Beverly Hills. It was the golden door of the Black community during the early 1900's and it proved that African Americans had successful infrastructure. That's what Black Wall Street was all about. The dollar circulated 36 to 100 times, sometimes taking a year for currency to leave the community. Now, a dollar leaves the Black community in 15 minutes. As far as resources, there were several Ph.D.'s residing in Little Africa, as well as Black attorneys and doctors.

One doctor was Dr. Berry, who owned the bus system. His average income was $500.00 a day, hefty pocket change in 1910. It was a time when the entire state of Oklahoma had only two airports, yet

44

six Blacks owned their own planes. It was a very fascinating community.

The area encompassed over 600 businesses and 36 square blocks with a population of 15,000 African Americans, and when the lower-economic Europeans looked over and saw what the Black community created, many of them were jealous. When the average student went to school on Black Wall Street, he wore a suit and tie, because of the morals and respect they were taught at a young age.

The main stay of the community was to educate every child. Nepotism was the one word they believed in, and that's what we need to get back to today. The main thoroughfare was Greenwood Avenue, and it was intersected by Archer and Pine Streets. From the first letters in each of those three names, you get G.A.P., and that's where the renowned R & B music group *The GAP Band* which is from Tulsa, got their name!

Black Wall Street was a prime example of the typical Black community in America that did business, but it was in an unusual location. You see, at the time, Oklahoma was set aside to be a Black and Indian state. There were over 28 Black townships there. One third of the people who traveled in the terrifying "Trail of Tears," alongside the Indians from 1830 to 1842, were Black people.

The citizens of this proposed Indian and Black state chose a Black governor, a treasurer from Kansas named McDade. But the Ku Klux Klan said that if he assumed office that they would kill him within 48 hours. A lot of Blacks owned farmland, and many of them had gone into the oil business. The community was so tight and wealthy because they traded dollars hand-to-hand, and because they were dependent upon one another as a result of the *Jim Crow* laws. It was not unusual that if a resident's home accidentally burned down, it could be   rebuilt within a few weeks by neighbors.  This was the type of scenario that was going on day-to-day on Black Wall Street.  When Blacks intermarried into the Indian culture, some of them received their promised *40 acres and a mule* and with that came whatever oil was later found on the properties.

To show you the wealth a lot of Black people had, there was a banker in a neighboring town who had a wife named *California Taylor*.  Her father owned the largest cotton gin west of the Mississippi River.  When California shopped, she would take a cruise to Paris every three months to have her clothes made.

There was also a man named Mason in nearby Wagner County, who had the largest potato farm on the Mississippi.  When he harvested, he would fill 100 boxcars a day.  Another brother not far away had the same thing with a spinach farm.  The typical family then was five children or more, though the typical farm family would have 10 kids or more, who made up the nucleus of the labor.

On Black Wall Street, a lot of global business was conducted.  The community flourished from the early 1900's until June 1, 1921.  That's when the largest massacre of non-military Americans in the history of this country took place, and it was led by the Ku Klux Klan.  Imagine walking out of your front door and seeing; 1,500 homes being burned.  It must have been amazing.

Black Wall Street reminds me of the island of *Atlantis*, because its innovation, creativity and advance technologies were far ahead of the technologies of the times.  I do believe there was an Atlantis viewed by the great Greek philosopher Plato.  I do believe the inhabitants of Atlantis were the Minoan civilization.

46

Atlantis was eventually destroyed by a nature tsunami; however, Black Wall Street was destroyed by a human tsunami and those responsible were the Anglo-Americans from Tulsa, Oklahoma, and the Ku Klux Klan. These groups created horror and devastation all over Black Wall Street, therefore ending the most prolific Black community in American History.

## Chapter Six

## The Jewish American Impact on the American Economy

The history of the Jews in the United States has been part of the American National Fabric since colonial times. Until the 1830's, the Jewish community of Charleston, South Carolina was the largest in North America.

Within the large scale immigration of Jews from Germany, in the 19th century, they established themselves in many small towns and cities. A much larger immigration of Eastern European Jews, 1880-1914 brought a large, poor, traditional element to New York City. Refugees arrived from Europe after World War II, and many arrived from the Soviet Union after 1970.

In the 1940's Jews comprised 3.7% of the national population. Today, the population is about 5 million (under 2% of the national total) and shrinking, because of small family sizes and intermarriage. The largest population centers are the metropolitan areas of New York (2.1 million in 2000), Los Angeles (668,000), Miami (331,000), Philadelphia (285,000), and Boston (254,000).

Like virtually every population group in the United States, Jews came to this country as immigrants, and like most of these groups, the Jews have gradually worked their way from the bottom of the economic heap to more comfortable positions in the middle, or even the top of the spectrum. It's a struggle that took decades of hard work on the part of millions of Jewish Americans, just as it did for the Irish American, and many other ethnic groups. -13

Today we see millions of Hispanic Americans from many countries in Latin America, as well as Asian Americans from countries such as Vietnam and Cambodia, immersed in the same struggle and with the same hope for eventual triumph.  Naturally, every American immigrant group has its unique characteristics.  In the case of the Jews, particularly those who came to the United States from the 1930', two special characteristics gave them an unusual economic and social status; on the one hand, many of them were fleeing from persecution: programs in Eastern Europe, discrimination in Western Europe and ultimately, the rise of genocidal anti-Semitism in fascist Germany and Italy.  This put them at an economic disadvantage as compared to some other immigrant groups.  Whereas Christian immigrants from say, Germany and Ireland, could maintain close ties to friends, families, and communities in the homeland, even traveling back and forth as circumstances dictated, Jews who were fleeing oppression had no such luxury.  They had to depend on their own resources in the new world, to sink or swim as fate dictated.

On the other hand, the flight from persecution also meant that the Jew who came to America included a larger-than-normal proportion of highly skilled, well educated, professional people.  A successful non-Jewish lawyer, professor or doctor in a country like France or Italy was not very likely to immigrate to the United States, since they probably already enjoyed a comfortable existence at home.

Those who did leave were more likely to be poor laborers, the unskilled or the semi-skilled, who had to develop themselves intellectually and educationally in order to succeed in America.

But for Jews in Europe, persecution recognized no boundaries of education status, and many of the Jews who fled to America were intellectually and professionally advanced.  Perhaps the most tragic statistics compiled by the Holocaust survivor's foundations suggest that about 25% of American survivors of the Holocaust are living in poverty (currently close to 30,000 people).  It's sad to think that, after all they've lived through; these individuals are unable to enjoy a comfortable and secure old age in their adopted homeland.

Thankfully, more fortunate members of the Jewish community take their obligations to the Jewish poor very seriously.  On a  national scale, the Jewish Foundations of North America, representing 157 Jewish Federations and 400 network communities, raise and distribute more than $3billion annually for social welfare, social services and educational needs, many of them targeted to the poor (both Jewish and non-Jewish).  The evidence seems clear: Jews may be 2% of the U.S. Population, but they are responsible for a lot more than 2% of the charitable giving.

The idea that Jews are prominent in business is one anti-Semitic myth that does have a glimmer of truth behind it. Jews have enjoyed success in the business world in numbers out of proportion to their share of the population.-14

History has shown that the exclusion of Jews from occupations other than finance and trade  made them experts in those fields, just as the emergence of modern capitalism was making them into some of the most lucrative and significant areas of endeavor. Furthermore, in fields like finance, where European Jews developed traditions and skills that they later imported to America, the prominence of Jews in the industry may be slightly exaggerated by the ubiquity of Jewish names in company logos.  Why? Again, exclusionary practices played a part until the 1970's; most of the great banking and investment companies on Wall Street wouldn't hire a Jewish associate, no matter how talented and brilliant.  In defense, the Jews started their own firms, which soon competed on an equal footing against those that hired gentiles. As a result, companies like *Goldman Sachs, Kuhn Loeb, Oppenheimer and Company, Lehman Brothers, and Lazard Freres* rose to international prominence; and the family names above the doors soon attracted attention, including scowls from anti-Semites whenever anything controversial happened in the world of high finance.

Much the same is true in other fields of business. Take Hollywood and the media in general, where one of the stock claims by anti-Semites is that Jews control the industry and manipulate it to the benefit of *their people*. Actually, when it comes to entertainment, the idea that Jews are unusually successful does have a grain of truth.  On Google, you can find a list of prominent Jews in the American media in about three seconds and the list is quite impressive: *Summer Redstone* and *Michael Eisner* to *Steven Spielberg* and *Larry King*. There's no denying Jews have made their mark in Hollywood.

*Ewing Marion Kaufman* (September 21, 1916 – August 1, 1993) was an American pharmaceutical magnate, philanthropist and Major League Baseball owner. Born near Garden City, Missouri, Kaufmann grew up in Kansas City, Missouri.  He was bedridden for a year at age 11 with a heart ailment, during which time he read as many as 40 books a month. Kaufmann was an Eagle Scout and, as an adult, was awarded the Distinguished Eagle Scout Award.

After serving in the United States Navy in World War II, Kaufmann worked as a pharmaceutical salesman until 1950, when he formed Marion Laboratories with a $5,000 investment, operating it initially out of the basement of his home.  He reportedly chose to use his middle name rather than his last name in order not to appear to be a one-man operation.

Marion Laboratories had revenues of $930 million the year before it merged with Merrell Dow Pharmaceuticals (now part of Aventis) in 1989. The company sales made more than 300 millionaires. *-15*

***Abraham Kuhn, Loeb & Co.*** – Kuhn, Loeb & Co. was a bulge bracket, investment bank founded in 1867 by Abraham Kuhn and Solomon Loeb. Under the leadership of Jacob H. Schiff, it grew to be one of the most influential investment banks in the late 19$^{th}$ and 20$^{th}$ centuries, financing America's expanding railways and growth companies, including Western Union and Westinghouse, and thereby becoming the principal rival of J.P. Morgan & Co. In the years following Schiff's death in 1920, the firm was led by Otto Kahn and Felix Warburg, men who had already solidified their roles as Schiff's able successors. However, the firm's fortune began to fade following World War II, when it failed to keep pace with a rapidly changing investment industry, where Kuhn, Loeb's old –world, genteel ways, did not seem to fit; the days of the gentleman-banker had passed. The firm lost its independence in 1977, when it merged with Lehman Brothers, to create Lehman Brothers, Kuhn, Loeb, Inc. The combined firm was acquired in 1984 by American Express, forming Shearson/Lehman/American Express and with that, the Kuhn Loeb name was lost forever. Kuhn Loeb is considered to be one of the last gentlemen investment houses.*-16*

# Chapter Seven

## Asian American Entrepreneurs and the American Economy

Asian American communities have flourished since the arrival of the new immigrant's in the U.S., starting after 1965. The growth of those ethnic economies is directly and intrinsically tied to the growth of Asian businesses. Walk around any China Town, little Tokyo, Korean Town, or Little Saigon and you'll see hundreds of small shops and businesses, selling everything from traditional foods, ethnic music, travel, haircuts and manicures, flowers and liquor. The United States Asian population is 3.6 % however; they represent 4.8% of American business. As it turns out, of all the major racial/ethnic groups, Asian Americans are the most likely to own their own small businesses (along with some European immigrants). As the results shows, foreign-raised Asians (those who immigrated to the U.S. at age 13 or older) are much more likely to be self-employed than U.S. raised Asians (those who are either U.S. born or who immigrated to the U.S. before age 13 – the "1.5" generation). -17

Among foreign-raised Asians, Koreans have the highest self-employment rates among the U.S.

In fact, research shows that in the last couple of decades, women immigrants and people of color have entered self-employment in increasingly larger numbers. The question then becomes, "why are so many Asian immigrants opening up their own business?" In my academic research on self-employment and entrepreneurship, I have identified four main categories. Of course, as with any categorization system, there will sometimes be some overlap between categories, but for the most part, they represent unique characteristics that are associated with being self-employed.

The first is the theory of **labor market discrimination**, which argues that immigrants try to find a **regular** job as an employee working for someone else, but can't, and therefore, have no choice but to go into business for themselves because:

- The immigrant is not very fluent in English.
- Their educational or occupational credentials are inadequate.
- Simple discrimination by the employer is based on race.

The best examples of this theory are the experiences of Chinese immigrants in the late 1800's. The second theory emphasizes **cultural traits or ethnic resources**. This theory says that when immigrants choose to go into business for themselves, they apply their cultural traditions of working hard, delaying material gratification and sacrificing for the next generation. They also rely on using family or other immigrants in their ethnic group as unpaid or cheap labor. Sometimes, they also set up an informal savings and loan arrangement with friends or relatives to get start-up capital. Common ethnicity helps them develop a network of loyal customers within their own ethnic group.

A third theory of Asian immigrant self-employment focuses on **class resources**. Here, Asian immigrants plan from the beginning to open their own business, using specific education and job skills gained just for that purpose. They are also likely to have lots of financial resources to help them start their businesses. Finally, they tend to have **Americanized** attitudes and norms of behavior that make it easier for them to relate to their Asian and non-Asian customers and community.

Finally, there is the theory of *structural opportunities*, which has three separate sub theories or *models*. The first is the middleman minority model. This model argues that middle and upper-class White business owners don't want to deal with their predominately Black or Latino working class customers, because they fear losing money, status or for their own personal safety. Therefore, they "use" Asian immigrants to serve as a buffer zone, while they still control wholesale and distribution and the Asian business owners are left to face the hostility that is ultimately directed at Whites.

The second model is that of the ethnic enclave. This argues that it is in the Asian immigrant owner's best interest to open their businesses within their own ethnic community or enclave, because the most developed enclaves (e.g. Chinatown in San Francisco and New York) then produce much more profits. Also, working in the ethnic enclaves shields owners and workers from racial hostility and discrimination that they would normally face in the mainstream labor market.

The last model within the structural opportunities theory focuses on economic openings as White small business owners sell their businesses in inner cities (e.g. Jews and Italians in New York in the 1980's), Asian immigrants take over in these areas. Also, as the U.S. economy changes from one based on manufacturing to services, more service-oriented business opportunities develop. These businesses tend to offer easy entry, but also involve high risks of losses or failures (e.g. garment, groceries, restaurants, personal services, and retail sales.)

## Chapter Eight

## Arab American Entrepreneur and Their Impact on the American Economy

An Arab American is a United States citizen or resident of Arab ethnic, cultural and linguistic heritage who identifies themselves as Arab. Arab Americans trace their ancestry to any of the various waves of immigrants of the countries comprising the Arab world. Americans descended from immigrants of the Arab world via other countries are also included. -18

Countries of origins for Arab Americans include Lebanon, Syria, Palestine (Gaza Strip and West Bank, plus Arab citizens of Israel), Jordan, Iraq, Saudi Arabia, Yemen, Oman, United Arab Emirates, Qatar, Bahrain, and Kuwait in West Africa and Morocco (plus Sahrawi's from disputed Western Sahara) Algeria, Tunisia, Libya, Northern Sudan and Egypt, in North Africa.

Arab Americans are considered an ethnic group and comprise approximately 1.5% of the population. Arab Americans and Arabs in general, comprise a highly diverse amalgam of groups with differing ancestral origins, religious backgrounds and historical identities. The ties that bind are a shared heritage by virtue of common linguistic, cultural and political traditions.

The majority of Arab Americans, around 62%, originate from the region of the Levant, which includes Syria, Lebanon, Palestine/Israel, and Egypt. The remainders are made up of those from Jordan, Iraq, Libya, Morocco, and other Arab nations, which are small in numbers, but present nonetheless. There are nearly 3.5 million Arab-Americans in the United States, according to the Arab-American Institute. Arab-Americans live in all 50 states and

Washington, D.C., and 94% reside in the metropolitan areas of major cities.

The Arab-American immigrant's first phase of earning a living was usually as a merchant of dry goods and notions, commonly called a **pack peddler**. The peddlers were married couples working together or singly, unmarried men or women, widowers or widows, and teenage boys. They traveled door to door to the outskirts of the city and surrounding towns by foot or by horse and buggy and out of state as far as the Midwest by foot or train. They worked for weeks or months at a time before returning home. Peddling was a carry-over from Ez-belaad, where it was a normal form of commerce. From the merchandising earnings, the immigrants established retail, wholesale or export-import businesses. They purchased real estate to rent, and they built residences and commercial residential buildings. Many invested successfully in the stock market and participated in community activities. [19]

In days of limited transportation, pack peddlers played an important function because the wares they sold provided the basic needs of their customers. A peddler filled a **Kushee** (box, trunk or suitcase) and or a gunny cloth, with the corners tied together, with dry goods and notions. They often carried rolled up oriental rugs over their backs and shoulders. Generally, the Arab American immigrant was a composite portrait of an adventure seeker, whose cheerful perseverance, commitment, fortitude, honesty, reliability, and resourcefulness helped in facing the many daily challenges of developing door-to-door sales routes in unfamiliar areas, and overcoming language barriers.

The peddler's driving force was to sell, earn money, raise a family, and preserve the family honor. The supportive structure of the biological and extended families influenced the immigrants' progress. In the extended family, certain members chose to work and assist in the family businesses, while others were free to venture to distant areas for work. The strong ties of family helped them achieve confidence, unity and purpose in search of the good life. Peddling enabled them to maintain their independence and earn beyond a set wage. It provided the freedom to expand and experiment without restrictions or supervisors. Elis reflected on his choice of livelihood: "I can't work for anybody. Nobody could ever tell me what to do. I've got to feel what I'm doing. I loved the challenge of selling from door to door. I love my work." After settling in Worchester, some immigrants continued their trek across the country as itinerant peddlers and then resettled in a place more to their liking. Frequently, however, they continued to consider Worchester friends by mail and visits.

The bakeries, restaurants, coffeehouses, and other establishments in the three Arab American neighborhoods, El-Tellee, Harrate - Tahta and lower Belmont Street, provided employment for the owners. These establishments also served as networking centers for exchange of business information and provided recreational and social activities for both local residents and out-of-towners. Here's a list of some prominent Arab American business leaders, below,

> *Steve Jobs, Co-founder of Apple Computers (Syrian Father, Abdulfattah Jandali)*

> *John Zogby, (Lebanese) Founder and current President/C.E.O. of Zogby Company.*

> *Jacques Nasser (Lebanese) Former President & C.E.O. of Ford Motor Company.*

> *John J. Mack (Lebanese) Chairman of the Board and C.E.O. of Morgan Stanley.*

## Chapter Nine

## The Reasons the African American Entrepreneur has Problems Growing Businesses in America

I will address several of the problems the African-American Entrepreneur has in developing and sustaining businesses in America. The following list is considered the three major problems for African Americans businesses' growth in America.

- The lack of understanding the basic concepts of business
- The lack of adequate capital to grow a business
- The lack of support in the African-American Community to support the African American Entrepreneur

### The Lack of Understanding the Basic Concepts of Business

Understanding and developing good business concepts has been difficult for the African American Entrepreneur; therefore, the need to discuss the reason is of utmost importance:

*The African American child does not have the same opportunity to learn business as other ethnic and Anglo children, due to a lack of existing business in the African American Community. Therefore, there is a need for a National Urban Minority Youth Entrepreneurship Initiative. This initiative would work with urban minority middle and high school students. This will allow urban youths to get exposure to entrepreneurship at a younger age, and would allow them the same basic business training as their counterparts. I believe this will increase African American entrepreneurship for young people for years to come...*

### The Lack of Adequate Capital to Grow a Business

The lack of venture capital, private equity and financing is prevalent in the African-American communities throughout America.

The lack of adequate capital to grow a business in the African-American Community has been a problem for a long time. Start-ups are difficult for any person, group or organization to develop, cultivate and grow. There are many reasons for this dilemma. Most African-American Entrepreneurs start with a great idea, but no capital.

Traditionally, most go to family or friends for assistance. Most people do not go to banks initially because their requirements for borrowing money are stringent. Banks require the following: a good track record, good credit, a good business plan, and some equity, so African-American Entrepreneurs start up with very *limited* amounts of capital resources.

Lack of venture capital is another reason African-Americans have traditionally had trouble acquiring or merging with others. Venture capital firms are associated with *job creation* accounting for 21% of U.S. (GDP), the knowledge economy, and used as a proxy measure for innovation with an economic sector or geography. Every year there are nearly 2 million businesses created in the U.S.A. and only 600-800 get venture capital funding. According to the National Venture Capital Association, 11% of the private sector jobs come from venture backed companies who are backed on revenue accounts for 21% of the U.S. GDP. A private equity investment will generally be made by a private equity firm, a venture capital firm or an angel investor. Each category of investors has its own set of goals, preferences and investment strategies. Each one provides working capital to target companies to nurture expansion, new product development or restructuring of the company's operations, management or ownership.

## Private Equity

Among the most common investment strategies in private equity are leveraged buyouts, venture capital, growth capital distressed investments, and maintenance capital. Private equity is defined by Wikipedia as an asset class consisting of equity securities in operating companies that are not publicly traded on the stock exchange. Venture capital is financial capital provided to early stage, high potential, high risk growth start up companies; so the questions is, "Why do African-Americans have trouble getting capital to develop their businesses, whereas, the other ethnic entrepreneurs get it from their family, friends or their communities?" *-20*

## King Pinning

It is important to understand the concept of groups putting their ***pennies, nickels and dimes*** together. One concept that is used in ethnic America is coined as ***King Pinning***.  The concept is a group of entrepreneurs get behind one person and make them the leader of the entrepreneurial project and finance the person, so that the leader's credit is good and they then have enough revenue to help the group succeed. It is a concept common among ethnic groups in America.

## The Lack of Support in the African-American Community to support the African American Entrepreneur

Lastly, the lack of support for African-American owned businesses by ***African Americans*** is a huge concern, due to the impact it has on African American employment.  I will address why this problem exists and render some solutions to vindicate those issues.

Historical data showed that prior to integration, business ownership and money was flowing through the African American community, dating back to the early twenties when Black Wall Street was booming. However, based on today's statistics and economy, the African-American money **turns** one time in the African American community. The term **turns** describes how many times *money is spent within the African-American community*. The concept is tied to spending with African-American owned businesses in and surrounding our community.

**Buying Black** has been a concept discussed, but not pursued in the African-American Community. The idea would be that "I" get paid and purchase the following from the African-American Entrepreneurs: groceries, clothes, cars, houses, legal and medical help, and etc. The concept is how many times "I" spend with African-American Entrepreneurs. The reasons that the lack of support is prevalent in today's economy and not during segregation are several. First, during segregation, Blacks lived in the same neighborhoods and, because of **Jim Crow** laws, many African-Americans were forced to purchase from African-American Entrepreneurs. However, today African-Americans are not in the same neighborhoods; therefore, purchasing from African-American Entrepreneurs is not a necessity anymore.

Next, some African-Americans do not want to see other African Americans achieve the American Dream, which in the African-American community is called the **crawfish** syndrome. The crawfish syndrome states that all crawfish are in one barrel and that they do not let one get out; and the motion the crawfish use is to pull the other crawfish climbing out back in with the rest of the crawfish.

It is an old wives' tale that has been passed down through the African-American community for generations. It means I do not want to see you get ahead; therefore, I will pull you back in the barrel with me. It is a concept that has to change if there is to be significant progress for the African-American Entrepreneur.

Finally, the African-American Entrepreneur has to be precise, diligent, hardworking and thrifty. The reasons are numerous; however, the old stereotypes still exist in the African-American community:

*Pricing goods and services are too high, goods are not repaired properly and good service is not provided to customers.*

These are the labels given to African-American Entrepreneurs. True or untrue, we need to again look at the **big picture**. I do believe African American Entrepreneurs can perform any and all tasks. However, both entrepreneur and client need to be consistent and persistent in looking at each given project to receive its desired results at the time.

In closing this chapter, we need to assess where we are and create goals to achieve the necessary objective of creating and increasing the number of African American Entrepreneurs.

*Chapter ten will discuss more in depth solutions to the venture capital and private equity dilemma or paradox along with ways to receive more venture capital and private equity firms within our community and create larger numbers of African American Entrepreneurs in America.*

## Chapter Ten: Some Solutions to the African American Entrepreneurial Experience

Last chapter, we discussed some of the reasons why the African America Entrepreneur has some problems in growing businesses in America. This chapter will deal with some solutions to the African American Entrepreneurial Experience.

Youth Entrepreneurship is one of the keys in developing more African American Entrepreneurs in America. Generation E Institute of Battle Creek, Michigan, is a Youth Entrepreneurship development program that operates all over the United States. I have excerpts from two founders, Dr. Kelly Moyers and Cheryl Peters, and their opinion of Urban Minority Youth development in Urban America.

✓   Why did you get involved with Youth Entrepreneurship?

**Cheryl Peters-Director-Generation E. Institute of Battle Creek, Michigan:**

As an educator for 20 years, I taught health and careers. At the middle school level, the career exploration program enables a student to discover their interests, talents and abilities. Students chose often by curiosity, a job field by the needed education and earning capacity – not by what they enjoyed or felt they had as a skill. Having owned my own business, I recognized the need to have *passion*. Without it, you don't have the needed drive.

I equally know it is essential to have an *understanding* of business to be a successful business owner. As I saw this gap in career exploration, I became interested in teaching entrepreneurship education. With an offer to explore this concept, I attended training and piloted a class. Being the curriculum developer and coordinator for my school district, I received approval to develop a curriculum for middle school career classes. The students grasped the concepts and created operational business ventures. Taking that interest to the next level, I became the coordinator of a local initiative to develop and expand youth entrepreneurship education. In collaboration with an intermediate school, the local community college and a community organization, I developed and piloted youth entrepreneurship educational courses for ages 10-26. The fact that young people could discover their interests and talents as they go through the beginning units and develop them into operational business ventures, learn business concepts, communication skills, and etc., inspires the Generation Institute to receive its nonprofit status.

**Dr. Kelly Moyers-Director-Generation E. Institute of Battle Creek Michigan:**

My interest in small business management and entrepreneurship began as I became an entrepreneur myself. I started a real estate investment company in 1994 in the Midwest. At that time it was a small, disorganized attempt at running a business. However, through reading the literature and my own experience, it became increasingly apparent that entrepreneurship was an important part of the community I lived in. I thought that, if this was the case, this must be an important part of all communities, in terms of economic growth and development. This sparked an interest in me to learn more about being a successful business owner, not only to improve my own bottom line, but to make an effort to identify the role that small businesses and entrepreneurial ventures play in a community. After a few years, I successfully grew my business and was able to see, after much trial and error, how critical entrepreneurship is to any community large or small. It was this insight that served as a motivating factor to learn as much as I could. Eventually, I decided to seek an MBA and Ph.D. so that I could enter the world of academia to teach others about the wonders of entrepreneurship. Since then, I have had the pleasure and the true blessing of being able to educate youth and young adults in this field.

✓ How important is entrepreneurship in America's future?

**Cheryl Peters – Director- Generation E Institute of Battle Creek, Michigan:**

Our country has left the industrial era and the time when large factories would provide people, with minimal education, the opportunity to make a comfortable living. Education is essential to economic security. However, critical to economic prosperity is new business creation and innovation. New ideas, creative thinking and problem solving are essential skills for the U.S. to remain a leader in the global market. America was founded by entrepreneurs, and encouraging innovation is paramount to our economy. With the loss of huge factories, our communities must reinvent themselves. Entrepreneurial thinking will create new ideas, new methodology and innovations that can be accomplished in any community. Our communication system allows for the opportunity to have a business anywhere and serve people globally. This culture of thinking must be developed and nurtured as we move ahead in our ever changing world.

**Dr. Kelly Moyers – Director- Generation E. Institute of Battle Creek, Michigan:**

Youth entrepreneurship has always been an important part of the changes taking place in our current economy. As President Obama works diligently to act as a change agent to improve the American economy and to include the American youth segment into the equation of solving issues that are affecting family incomes and family futures, we are being positively encouraged to continue the work of educating our youth and young adults to be contributing and critical members as an answer to our needs, as a nation, to solve the current economic crisis we face. Towards that end, youth and young adults are becoming more and more relevant in how we plan and process the path to economic security. As an educator, my interest has only strengthened and grown, over the past decade, as we witness the many positive impacts that successful entrepreneurs are having on our country and its role as a global leader. With effective support and planning of their efforts, their important role will continue to grow as integral function towards economic development and success.

✓ Why do you think Urban Youth need to learn and develop entrepreneurial skills?

**Cheryl Peters – Director – Generation E Institute of Battle Creek, Michigan:**

All youth need to learn and develop entrepreneurial skills and a mindset to successfully compete in today's world. Many youth, brought up in an urban setting, do not come to school with the necessary skills to feel engaged in education. Young people, who are not secure at home, can hardly feel secure in a public environment. If they don't feel engaged and they struggle with core objects, the danger increases for student drop outs and for inappropriate behaviors. Entrepreneurship education causes all youth to feel that their ideas have value, their input is needed and their expertise and work will glean rewards. As youth learn entrepreneurial skills and develop business ideas, they see the relevance of core subjects. Math, English and communication skills are essential for business success. As they continue on this path towards business creation, the outside negative influences are not as strong. Once you have changed that culture of thinking, you have changed the focus of the youth.

**Dr. Kelly Moyer – Director- Generation E Institute of Battle Creek, Michigan:**

With a relatively high rate of poverty in many urban youth areas of the country, a comparatively high proportion of youth can benefit from learning entrepreneurial skills in an effort to successfully overcome economic, educational and social barriers. These learned skill sets include soft job skills such as effective communication, leadership, time management, team building and numerous other skills that are completely relevant to every aspect of life and are transferable to most careers in any industry. Students also learn the hard sciences, including math and science, financial literacy, business planning, and human resources, the lifelong skills they'll be using their whole lives, but just don't know it yet!

✓ What is the most important concept developed by youth entrepreneurs after learning entrepreneurship skills?

**Cheryl Peters – Director – Generation E Institute of Battle Creek, Michigan:**

Having the belief in yourself that you can accomplish something is essential for success in the world of work. Learning entrepreneurial skills, in conjunction with building upon one's own idea, is not only engaging, but very empowering. Youth become engaged in entrepreneurship education because they are getting to act on their idea. As they learn the necessary skills, they are empowered to problem solve, make decisions, evaluate situations, and know that the success of their business is in their hands. Youth rise to the challenge and those experiences build upon their character, self-confidence and the ability to express themselves as leaders in the world of work.

**Dr. Kelly Moyers – Director- Generation E Institute of Battle Creek, Michigan:**

Hands down, the most important concept youth learn through taking part in entrepreneurship education is discovering that they can do anything they set their minds to. No matter how distant and impossible it may seem when they begin, they learn to believe in themselves and their abilities, as well as to believe in their dreams coming true. Once this is instilled in a person, the other barriers, such as money, time and resources seem much easier to conquer. It's a life lesson that builds on their character and stays with them throughout life. It doesn't get much better than truly believing in yourself and showing the world that they should believe in you, too!

**Dr. Ron Evans President of the National Business League has offered some opinions on African American Business**

1.  **How has the African American business developed after 1964 Civil rights laws were passed?**

Many new and old businesses were enhanced through programs developed during the Nixon administration with the creation of the office of Minority Business Enterprises offices of the U. S. Department of Commerce now MBDA (Minority Business Development Agency). These programs brought attention to the developing communities of our nation; thus, the creation of organizations such as "Black Enterprise Magazine" and utilization of the U.S. Small Business Administration (SBA) and the use of the Section 8 (a) contracting opportunities; some of the benefactors of this program in the Washington, D.C. area were Colonel Theodore Adams, Verle Hammond, Rodney Hunt, and Sam Metters. This was made possible through the efforts of the Honorable Parren J, Mitchell, the first African American congressman from the state of Maryland. It was his untiring and relentless efforts to help minority business succeed. He pioneered the passage of Public Law 95-507; it was during this period that many African American businesses were allowed to contract with the U.S. Government agencies, for example, the Department of Defense, The Department of Agriculture, and The Government Services Administration (GSA), The Department of Energy (DOE), and many others. Since these programs were such a great success, they were subsequently watered down by the inclusion of other minority groups and women. Thus, the majority community began giving ownership majority to their wives and children. In order to participate in these programs, they were encouraged to form joint ventures and teaming agreements with majority firms to assure success in providing services and manufactured goods to the government, thus not a *handout, but a hand up*.

## 2. How were African American entrepreneurs doing prior to the Civil Rights laws of 1964?

Prior to the Civil Rights Laws being enacted, the African American business community strived for success through the typical "mom and pop" business orientation, along with a few who expanded their business opportunities within their respective business communities. For examples, *Dr. A.G. Gaston*, a former president of the NBL; he was an entrepreneur with a savings and loan association, funeral home and other ancillary businesses serving his immediate community of Birmingham, AL; *Horace Studduthe* a hotel business man in Cincinnati, OH another past president of the NBL; *Dr. Berkley G. Burrell*, another former president of the NBL; with his cleaning establishments; *Theodore R. Hagan*, another past president of the NBL, a hotel owner who became a real estate developer, could continue by bringing in *Dr. Frederick Patterson*, another past president of the NBL and the founder of the United Negro College Fund who coined the slogan *A Mind Is A Terrible Thing to Waste*.  Maybe we became our own worst enemy when they allowed us to integrate areas of our cities, we *abandoned* our own communities. Others who were successful prior to the Civil Rights Bill were people like; *Jesse Terry*, Terry Manufacturer, Alabama; *Dempsey J. Travis*, Mortgage banker, Chicago, *Edward Davis*, first Black new car dealer, Detroit, MI; *A. Otis Smith*, gas station proprietor; New York City, NY, *John W. Winters*, home-building contractor, Raleigh, NC; *Henry G. Parks, Jr.*, sausage manufacturer; Baltimore, MD; *Frederick E. Barrett*, electronic equipment manufacturer, Philadelphia, PA; *Asa T. Spaulding*, North Carolina Mutual Life Insurance Co. Durham, NC; and *Johnson and*

*Johnson Publishing Co.*, Chicago, IL. These are just a few additional business persons who succeeded prior to the Civil Rights Bill, which may or may not have been a blessing to the African American Community.

Most African American businesses today are concentrated in the areas of personal services and small retail operations. As we look at other national organizations, we find a lessening of their influence, since the major American organizations are now accepting us as members; like realtors, medical association, architects, bankers and others.

3.   **What programs helped African American entrepreneur's develop their business the most?**

Prior to the Civil Rights laws and integration, we worked in our communities with one another. The National Business League, The National Urban League and the NAACP, had significant impact on the African American community; bringing attention to the disparities in the community, for example, health issues, job development, housing ownership and business development.

4.   **How do you see youth entrepreneurship helping to develop future entrepreneurs?**

The youth Entrepreneurship programs may bring more of our youth to the understanding of business and realize the importance of owning and operating their own businesses, as opposed to building business for the majority of the community. This will give our youth and future leaders the opportunity to provide employment in their communities. Mentorship training with the introduction of business acumen at a very early age, from K through Middle school, will benefit the African American community in the future. I am encouraged by the national Business League Urban Youth

Entrepreneurship Program (NBLUYEP) concept, for it will provide future leadership for the African American community as a whole. The most successful businesses are started with the desire to be one's own boss at a very early age. I, myself began a small business by handing out 3x5 cards with my information on them, providing a delivery and messenger service to the residents of the projects that I grew up in; then I had a newspaper route, working for others to learn how they did business and also working with my family in their accounting and tax services business.

5. **Do you feel that venture capital and private equity can help African American entrepreneurs develop their business?**

Venture capital can have a positive impact as well as a negative impact on the African American business. It worked effectively until we were unable to maintain control of the businesses that found themselves totally reliant upon outside investors who controlled and wanted to direct the operation of the business. Thus, causing a total loss of control by the entrepreneur, who was the creator that developed the company from their own concepts, ideas and or designs? A prime example is when a person has invented a product, obtained the patents on same and was forced to give up all interest to a majority of investors, who then would take control of the development of the product, concept or idea.

## 6. How do you view the future development of the African American business?

When we decide to come together as a people, then and only then will we see growth and development in our communities. Our saving grace today will be the development of our youth to become entrepreneurs and become self-sufficient, provide employment and maintain control of their own destiny.

In the last chapter we discussed another area that deserves some attention when it comes to the economic empowerment of African-American Entrepreneurs. The concept was venture capital and private equity; retire Professor Timothy Bates of Wayne State University and William Bradford of the University of Washington. They give us insight into the history and development of venture capital and private equity for African American Entrepreneurs.

From its inception in 1970 through the early 1990's, the segment of the venture capital industry that financed Minority Business Enterprises (MBEs) relied upon government sponsors for funding and directions. Nearly all of the minority-oriented venture capital funds were chartered by the U.S. Small Business Administration (SBA) and operated within its regulatory framework itself; over the past decade, the minority venture capital industry has transformed itself, largely shedding its reliance upon SBA funding while adopting the organization framework the partnership of the mainstream industry.

In the 1990s another branch of the minority venture capital industry arose that was funded largely by public pension funds. Our comparative analysis of the SBA and Pension Fund branches of the Venture Capital Industry indicates that the former is stunted while the latter is thriving. Our analysis indicates that the SBA is too unstable an agency for promoting the minority venture capital industry. In contrast to the SBA's propensity to alter policy based on shifting political priorities, the pension funds have been a stable, reliable source of support for the growing minority venture capital industry.

The birth of the minority-oriented venture capital industry traces back to President Nixon's first Urban Initiative, project enterprises, which was launched by executive order on November 6, 1969. One result was the creation, in 1970, of the Minority Enterprise Small Business Investment Company (MESBIC) Program. MESBICs were privately owned investment companies, chartered by the SBA, devoted to investing patient capital, venture capital and long term debt in Black owned business. By 1972 the MESBIC mandate had been expanded to "facilitate capital formation in the minority community." In practice, capital was extended largely to Black and Hispanic-owned firms, as well as a few nonminority-owned businesses that operated in urban minority communities.

Minority-oriented venture capital funds have a mandate to invest largely in minority owned businesses. Conceptually, the expected financial results for these venture capital funds depend significantly on whether or not minority-owned firms have full access to venture capital funding; that is whether majority venture capital investors provide sufficient capital to minority owned ventures. If minority-owned firms are treated as favorably in financial markets and have less access to venture capital than similarly situated majority businesses. The above average returns /below average risks may be available to venture capital funds focused on financing minority owned firms. There is available evidence describing access to venture capital than non-minority owners having similar human-capital traits. If this is indeed true, the minority-oriented venture capital firms should achieve favorable returns in the MBE niche, because there are unmet opportunities available.

The unmet opportunities that are available would be met if more African American athletes and entertainers would invest in venture capital and private equity funds. The athletes and entertainers would create profits for their investments and also help create more viable African American enterprises; thus, creating stronger urban communities, providing jobs and increasing the tax base in many urban markets around the United States; therefore, helping the urban area to provide better education and various other needed services in urban America.

With this book, my goal was to illustrate the following: African Americans need to look at other ethnic business success stories that were basically created years ago by other ethnic groups by simply putting their **pennies, nickels and dimes together**. I've included some helpful suggestions and solutions to the paradox in the African American economy.

# FOOTNOTE PAGE

1. Wikipedia, Economic status of African Americans, Why Africans Americans and other groups remain poor.
2. A story of Black Entrepreneurship, by Aaron Bocage and George Waters, pgs. 24, 25, 26
3. Wikipedia Paul Cuffee
4. Wikipedia Madam CJ Walker
5. A.G. Gaston
6. Wikipedia , Booker T. Washington delivers the 1895 Atlanta Comprise Speech
7. Wikipedia, Booker T. Washington & W.E.B DuBois, The Nations of Black America
8. Wikipedia, ( The Free Encyclopedia) The National Business League
9. Wikipedia ( The Free Encyclopedia )The National Urban League
10. The Negro Leagues (1869-1960) by Leslie A. Heaphy, McFarland & Company, Inc., Publishers, pgs. 39,77,78,79,80,81,211,212,213,221,223,224,225,226,228,229.
11. Black Wallstreet by Jay Jay Wilson & Ron Wallace, Seaburn Publishing Group, pgs 17, 18.
12. Wikipedia, (Black Wallstreet: The True Story)
13. Wikipedia, ( The Free Encyclopedia) The Jewish American History
14. Jews & Money The Story of a Stereotype by Abraham H. Foxman pgs 84,85,86,87,88,90,91,92,93,94,95.
15. Wikipedia (The Free Encyclopedia ), Arab American
16. Ewing Kaufmann
17. Abraham Kuhn & Solomon LOEB
18. Arab American Faces & Voices by Elizabeth Boosahda, pgs. 65, 66,77,2003, University of Texas Press, Austin
19. Wikipedia , (The Free Encyclopedia) Asian Small Businesses & Self Employment
20. Wikipedia, ( The Free Encyclopedia) Private Equity & Venture Capital

21. The Viability of the Minority-oriented Venture Capital Industry under Alternative Financing Arrangements. Timothy Bates, Wayne State University & William Bradford, University of Washington, pgs.3,,4,6,7.

22. "Getting It Together, Black Business In America" by John Sedert Berkeley G. Burrell ISBN 0-15-135275-5;l. of Catalog #70-142096

23. "The Need in Business" by Booker T. Washington Stories of Successful Entrepreneurs Original Copyright, 1907, By Hertel, Jenkins& Co;@1992 Devore& Sands Inc.

24. "Apiece of the Pie" BY Peter Fretty & Shelton P. Rhodes, PHD. ISBN-10:1-59800-003-9: ISBN-13:978-1-59800-003-OLOFC. Catalogue #:2005924415; A Book That Profiles Four African American Entrepreneurs in The Washington Area that are products of the 8(a) programs doing business with the U.S. government.

25. "The Inventive Spirit of African Americans" by Patricia Carte Sluby: ISBN 0-275-96674-7;L of C. Catalogue card #2003064767

## About the Author

**King L. Taylor Jr.** is an author, entrepreneur and educator who reside in St. Louis, Missouri. He began his journey at Park University of Kansas City, Missouri where he received his undergraduate degree in Business Administration Economics. Mr. Taylor's expertise began to flourish while working for Dial Corporation and The Hartz Mountain Corporation in management. He went on to receive his master's degree in Management from Fontbonne University in St. Louis, Missouri. Mr. Taylor has been involved in several entrepreneurial endeavors including manufacturing, distribution and retail operations. He is the recipient of the *Mass Mutual Blue Chip Enterprise Award*; and for the past several years he has served as vice president of the National Business League in his region.